Matu Reading Instruction

LEVEL 3

Piper
Books

Introduction

'The human brain seems to be set up specially for the retention of stories. They sink in and they stay in the mind more easily than anything else. Things that create an emotional reaction will be better remembered.'

- Daniel Willingham, 'Why Don't Students Like School?'

MRI (Mature Reading Instruction) offers a complete reading program within a framework of highly structured stories which start off very simply and soon develop into darker, more morally complex tales suitable for teenagers and adults. They offer numerous opportunities to explore age-old yet extremely relevant issues of identity, morality, prejudice, religion, free will, etc. The stories are abridged versions of many of the great works of English literature, and myths and legends from around the world. The program is based on the phonics principles repeatedly shown to be the most successful method of teaching reading – especially for the 'problem' students who have fallen through the educational net. Those who suffer from genuine learning difficulties like dyslexia will find their brains 'retrained' by Systematic Synthetic Phonics. And those who fell behind due to confusing mixed teaching methods and/or an insufficiency of practice will finally get the consistency, controlled exposure and varied repetition they need. This will lead to automatic decoding, which in turn results in confidence, fluency and greater comprehension.

Accompanying the five Levels of MRI is a comprehensive Tutor Guide, including Practical Teaching Points, Initial and Final Assessments, Background Information About the Stories, Record Keeping, Fluency Practice, Copying and Dictation Exercises, Frequently Asked Questions, and Troubleshooting.

Instruction

Instruction is very straightforward:

Before embarking on each story, practice each letter/sound it introduces.

The only instruction the student needs is 'Say the sounds and read the word.'

When the student is stuck for more than a few seconds, just point to the letter/sound correspondence in question and say: 'The sound here is "_____".'

Insist on accurate reading at all times: each person differs but each must learn to handle the same Alphabetic Code.

Don't allow guessing – it is a very difficult habit to eradicate.

Avoid explanations, hints, and other 'help'.

Ensure that attention is paid to 'reading through the word' – in particular with word endings.

Encourage rereading of earlier books with expression.

Discuss the stories afterwards to develop speech, language and vocabulary.

Contents

PLAY 1

Hammer of the Gods

'Hammer of the Gods' based on the Norse legend of Thor's Hammer.

Introducing:

Grapheme 'y', sound /ee/ (*merry, funny, dishy…*)
Suffix 'ly' (*restlessly, endlessly, likely…*)

Hammer of the Gods

The days went by, for gods and ice-trolls and men alike.

The fate of them all had long been foretold:

'The Endless Winter will come. Gods and ice-trolls will clash in the Last Combat of Ragnarok. The world will perish in fire.'

But all that was yet to come…

* * * * *

Time after time, Skoll the Wolf raced Sol the Sun across the sky, in an endless dance.

All the while, Fenric stayed bound to his rock, snapping and growling and cursing the gods who'd tricked him. How he longed for Ragnarok!

The Serpent stirred restlessly in his sleep under the waves, killing mariners by the dozen.

At Midgard, home of mankind, inhabitants worked endlessly to produce crops, blessed by the goddess Freya. Miners dug gold – the outcome of Freya's weeping – from the dust and dirt of the mines. Lads and lasses wed, blessed by the goddess Var. Men perished in combat, and the gates of the underworld opened for them.

At Asgard, home of the gods, Thor waved his massive hammer and Saga told tales. Sif tossed her long golden locks and Balder smiled sweetly. Odin gazed at a fresh lover, and his wife Freya gazed at *him*, gritting her teeth. Loki plotted his next trick.

And, needless to say, the trolls in the ice-caves plotted to bring down the gods.

All was normal, or as normal as life ever got under The World-Tree.

Until the day came that the ice-trolls plotted no longer.

They acted.

* * * * *

THOR [*thundering*]: LOKI! Get over here, you vile trickster –

LOKI [*pouting*]: Who, me? What have I done *this* time?

THOR: Where – is – my – hammer! Give it back to me this second and *if* you're lucky I *may* desist from ripping you to shreds –

LOKI: Hey! Put me down! I didn't swipe that hammer, okay? I may like to play the odd trick but do you think I'm *nuts*? You waving that thing around is all that keeps us gods safe from the ice-trolls –

He stops.

LOKI and THOR: Hell's bells! *The Ice-Trolls!*

LOKI: Okay. Do not panic. Stop making it thunder, you'll bring the sky down on us! I'll go and have a nice gossip with the Troll King, okay? See what info I can turn up. Wish me luck... back in a tick!

LOKI turns into an owl to fly to Utgard, land of the ice-trolls.

TROLL KING: Hey, my old pal Loki! Long time no see! How's tricks?

LOKI: Oh, fine, thanks… just fine… hey, something funny happened to old Thor today –

TROLL KING [*flatly*]: You want me to tell you where we hid the hammer.

LOKI [*taken aback*]: Er… yes. That'd be… nice of you.

TROLL KING: Nine miles down. Where no god will find it. Ever.

LOKI: Okay, not *that* nice of you. Can I offer you something to get it back?

TROLL KING: Funny you say that. As it happens, there IS something I want.

LOKI: Oh…? Do tell!

TROLL KING: Freya.

LOKI: *Freya?*

TROLL KING: Yup, Freya. Most dishy of the gods. Foxy… classy… stunning… *that* Freya.

LOKI: That… um… may be a bit tricky.

TROLL KING: Are you not a trickster?

LOKI: I'll… er… see what I can do.

TROLL KING: Thanks, buddy! Do come to the wedding! You can even be my best man!

LOKI returns to Asgard, home of the gods.

THOR: Tell me you've found a way to get my hammer back!

LOKI: Yes, um, no, um, well, kind of… That is to say, the Troll King will give it back… *if* Freya becomes his bride.

THOR [*gleefully*]: That's ALL? Fantastic! Well done, Loki!

LOKI: Thor, just hang on a sec –

THOR: Forget what I've been saying for… well… *forever*… about you being a bit of a baddy –

LOKI [*snorting*]: Whatever.

THOR: You are *fantastic*! A credit to the gods! Let's go tell Freya! Speed her on her merry way!

LOKI: Thor… you don't think there may be a small… snag?

THOR: *Snag*?

LOKI: Freya is, um, not likely to be that happy at wedding a troll. Brutish… ugly… lumpen… ringing any bells? Gods and trolls do not tend to mix… um, well, *most* of the time…

THOR: Yes, we're all well aware that *you'll* be on the ice-trolls' side, come the Last Days of Ragnarok, you total and utter –

LOKI [*sadly*]: That 'Loki is fantastic' stuff didn't last long, did it?

THOR: We'll just have to *make* her wed!

LOKI: Sunshine… do *not* be tricked by that sweetness-and-roses stuff Freya puts on to impress the mortals. The girl has massive power. And a nasty temper. She also – you seem to have forgotten – has a husband. Odin… king of the gods… maker and ruler of the cosmos… am I ringing any bells, here…?

THOR: Loki… *I need that hammer.* I'll need it at Ragnarok. I need it now. It's my power, my life, my destiny –

LOKI: Yes, yes, whatever. Hey, perk up – I have a cunning plan…

LOKI tells THOR his plan.

THOR: How dare you! Go jump in the lake! Who do you think you are? Who do you think *I* am – an unmanly *coward*?

LOKI: What happened to 'my power, my life, my destiny'...?

THOR: To hell with destiny! No *way*!

LOKI: So... do you want to tell Freya you're selling her to a troll, or shall I...?

THOR [*sobbing*]: Okay, okay! I'll go along with this 'cunning plan'. But if you even *think* of sniggering at me –

LOKI [*grinning*]: Who, me?

Three days later, at the TROLL KING's hall at Utgard:

LOKI: Oh King of the Ice-Trolls – behold! Here comes the goddess of love, spring and crops, Freya herself, to wed you! In return for Thor's hammer, that is!

ALL TROLLS: Greetings! Greetings! Greetings!

TROLL KING [*smugly*]: Welcome, my bride! Oh,

what lovely golden locks! How tall and strong you seem, under the mask and all those dresses and necklaces! A fit wife for a troll! How lucky am I!

LOKI: She thanks her beloved husband.

TROLL KING [*gleefully*]: Come sit with me! Dine and drink to a long and happy wedlock, my foxy goddess!

'FREYA' sits, and behind her mask gulps down an ox, nineteen big fish and three vats of beer.

TROLL KING: Never have I seen a bride who ate an entire ox! Is my darling feeling okay?

LOKI: For three days the goddess has fasted, so strong was her wish to meet you!

TROLL KING: Oh, how I have longed for her also! I'll just peek under that mask to see her sweet face – aaaaahh! Her glare! It's lucky it didn't turn me to rock!

LOKI: Ah, forgive the sweet bride… for three days

her longing for you has given her no rest, no sleep!

TROLL KING: Ah, bless! But why is she so silent? Have I offended her in some way?

LOKI: Never! She's just a bit shy in the face of her vast love for you.

TROLL KING: Oh my darling! I'll make you so happy you'll be jeering at that ex-husband Odin within the week!

LOKI: Just see her nod in agreement! Oh, and by the way… the bride-offering you vowed to her…?

TROLL KING: Oh, that silly hammer of Thor's! Here you go, my pet! Do with it what you will!

'FREYA': Thanks, my darling!

'FREYA' embeds the hammer in the TROLL KING's skull.

TROLL KING: Ow!

'FREYA' rips off her mask and golden wig.

'FREYA': For I am Thor the God of Thunder! And with this hammer in my hands I can slay all the trolls in this hall, no problem!

ALL TROLLS: Eek! Not *Thor*! Run for the hills!

GLOSSARY

~

ASGARD: homeland of the gods.

BALDER: ODIN's son; best-loved of all the gods; will be killed by his brother HOD thanks to LOKI.

BOR: ODIN's father; wed to an ICE-TROLL.

FENRIC (also called FENRIS): massive wolf, bound to a rock by the gods. RAGNAROK will come when he frees himself and kills ODIN.

FREYA (also called FRIGG): goddess of love, spring, and crops; wife of ODIN. Men killed in combat go to FREYA's Hall when they do not go to VALHALLA. Friday is named for her.

HEL: grim hag, part-alive, and part-carcass. Ruler of a hell for evil-doers and those who perished of sickness or infirmity, not combat.

HOD: blind god; will kill his beloved twin BALDER, thanks to LOKI's tricks.

ICE-TROLLS: massive, brutish opponents of the gods.

LOKI: god of fire; cunning, impish trickster. Will be bound to rocks by the gods for killing BALDER, and will command the trolls in the Last Combat with the gods. Father to FENRIC, HEL, the MIDGARD SERPENT and plenty more.

MIDGARD: the lands of mankind; a massive fortress made by the gods to protect men from the ICE-TROLLS.

MIDGARD SERPENT: vast and vile snake. When RAGNAROK comes, he will shake the lands and the deeps, and kill – and be killed by – THOR.

NORNS: goddesses of destiny; three sisters who

control the fates of gods and men.

ODIN (also called WOTAN): king of the gods and of VALHALLA; maker of the cosmos; god of combat and of wisdom. Husband to FREYA; father to THOR, BALDER, VIDAR, SAGA, and plenty more. Wednesday is named for him.

RAGNAROK: the foretold end of this cosmos; the Last Combat between ICE-TROLLS and gods. After three endless winters, all the lands will burn and then sink under the waves.

RAN: goddess of storms; ruler of perished mariners.

SAGA: goddess of history and the arts.

SKOLL: the wolf who will gulp down the sun, come RAGNAROK.

SIF: THOR's wife, famed for vanity and her long golden locks.

SOL: sun goddess; hunted across the sky by the wolf SKOLL.

SURT: lord of the fire-trolls, who will set fire to the WORLD-TREE itself, when RAGNAROK comes.

THOR: god of thunder; defender of gods and men; SIF's husband. THOR will kill and be killed by the MIDGARD SERPENT, when RAGNAROK comes. Thursday is named for him.

TIR: god of justice; has his left hand bitten off by FENRIC.

UTGARD: homeland of the ICE-TROLLS.

VALHALLA (also called VALHALL): the underworld. Those killed in combat end up in ODIN's VALHALLA; the rest go to FREYA's Hall or hell.

VALI: ODIN's son; will slay HOD to repay him for killing BALDER.

VAR: goddess of weddings.

VIDAR: during RAGNAROK, he will slay FENRIC for killing his father ODIN.

WORLD-TREE, The: colossal ash-tree that links and shelters all places in the cosmos, from ASGARD to MIDGARD. At its base are wells of wisdom and fate.

STORY 1

Baba Yaga

'Baba Yaga' based on the Russian folk tale of that name.

Introducing:

Grapheme 'ch', sound /ch/ (*cheese, enchantress, chicken...*)
Grapheme 'tch', sound /ch/ (*witch, watch, catch...*)

Words that may not be wholly decodable at this stage:

d oe s

Baba Yaga

~

Vasilisa and her father had a happy life together. Then the old man wed for a second time.

Bad, BAD mistake.

Within the week, her step-ma was simply fed up with small Vasilisa. Just see that merry grin! That pretty face! That sweet temper! The love and trust between the girl and her father! It was sick-making! The kid *had* to go!

And it didn't take long to think of a way. So, the moment the old man had set off to visit chums, the cunning plan was put into effect:

STEP-MA: Vasilisa! We're all out of ketchup!

VASILISA: *Ketchup?*

STEP-MA: Yes, I love the stuff, can't live without it. Go and ask my sister, Baba Yaga, for a big jar of ketchup.

VASILISA [*boggling in horror*]: sister?

STEP-MA: Problem?

VASILISA: *The* Baba Yaga?

STEP-MA [*smugly*]: That's the name.

VASILISA: Baba Yaga the *witch?*

STEP-MA: How dare you label my darling sister in such a way! Witch, indeed! That wicked mouth needs washing out!

VASILISA: Beg pardon, step-ma, but… she happens to be Baba Yaga the, er, hag? No, no, sorry! The… ah… skinny-legged enchantress? Baba Yaga who lives in a hut with chicken's feet and skulls? Famed for, um, spells and power…? Baba Yaga with the steel teeth? Oh, I'll say it… Baba Yaga who GULPS DOWN CHILDREN FOR DINNER?

STEP-MA [*grinning widely*]: You may think that, but I cannot possibly comment.

VASILISA: But… but…

STEP-MA: Oh, stop but-ing and be off with you!

VASILISA: But how will I find her?

STEP-MA: Turn left at the fallen ash-tree, go along the forest path for six miles, and lo and behold! There's my sister's chicken-legged hut! She'll be so happy to see you! Do try to get there by dinner-time!

VASILISA: *Dinner-time?*

STEP-MA: Here are some sandwiches to keep you going in case you get hungry on the way! Gosh, what a nice mother I am to you! Now stop crying and just get outta here, will you?

So Vasilisa lifted her chin and set off to meet her fate.

* * * * *

As Vasilisa's feet dragged along the path, she spotted a hanky on the ground. So she picked it up – it'd come in useful, what with her nose still dripping from all the crying.

Then, a mile or three later, Vasilisa spotted a ribbon. Well, when you are about to get *munched up by a witch*, finding a nice ribbon isn't much of a thrill, but what the heck – she may as well pick it up. And stare at it for a moment… a prized extra moment of life…

Then there was the pot of lard. 'Who'd drop a pot of lard in the trees?' asked Vasilisa aloud, forgetting the impending horror for a second.

But Vasilisa's life was ticking by… rushing to its bitter end…

Now time had run out and she was standing before the wall of bones and skulls…

… She was lifting the latch of the skull-gate…

… The gate made a shrill, sharp sound as it grated open.

'Oh, for pity's sake!' Vasilisa snapped, before whipping out her pot of lard, and rubbing the fat into the latch and springs of the gate.

Then she went inside.

* * * * *

There was Baba Yaga's hut, strutting around the yard on big chicken's legs… just as the tales said…

And there was Baba Yaga's slave-girl, standing sobbing in the yard.

'Whatever is the matter?' Vasilisa asked.

'Baba Yaga has – *hic*! – set me such tasks! I don't think I can do them all!' the slave gulped.

Vasilisa patted her kindly and handed her the

hanky. She held back from screeching, 'So you think *you've* got problems!'

She stepped boldly up to the hut. Outside a thin dog barked. 'Hungry?' Vasilisa asked, and tossed the dog the crusts from the cheese sandwich that her step-ma had given her. The dog wolfed them down and licked his lips.

Vasilisa stepped past the dog and went into the hut. At last, she was face-to-face with Baba Yaga! With the hag of a hundred tales: the vile, skinny-legged, child-muncher…

'Well, well, wench! Do come in! Fancy you just turning up here! Most times I have to fly out and hunt… er, lure… um, catch… ah! *invite*, children to visit me! What brings you here?'

'My st-step-ma,' stammered Vasilisa, feeling silly as well as ill-fated, 'told me to come here to her sister and get… er… er… er… ketchup.'

'Ha ha ha ha!' screeched Baba Yaga. 'Yes, that's my sister! So funny! So fond of ketchup! I'll go and fetch a jar! While you're here, I'm sure you'd like to be of use… did you see my spinning-wheel on the porch? Go out there and spin for me, will you?'

So Vasilisa meekly went and sat on the porch bench, and spun her last moments away… while Baba Yaga's thin black cat stared at her.

'Slave!' snapped Baba Yaga to the girl with Vasilisa's hanky, 'Get out the old tin bath, fill it up and scrub that wench! Can't have my dinner dirty when I munch her down – don't want to get ill! Pity my sister didn't find me a fatter child – there's not much flesh on her bones.'

'I beg you!' Vasilisa hissed to the girl as she went to and fro between the well in the yard and the kitchen fire with buckets and jugs, 'Take some time with the bath, for my life's sake!'

And the slave-girl bit her lip… but nodded, and dropped a jug in the fire.

Then Vasilisa asked the black cat how it was doing.

'Badly,' hissed the cat, jumping up onto the bench. 'No mice or rats for *three days*!'

And Vasilisa got the cheese filling from her sandwich, and fed it to the cat.

CAT [*purring*]: Yum-yum! Nice. By the way… Baba Yaga is planning on munching you up with her steel teeth today… Hey, stop howling! I can help!

VASILISA: How? *How?*

CAT: See the hairbrush and the towel by the bath? Grab them and run!

VASILISA: That's *it?*

CAT: Well, I'll take over the spinning so Baba Yaga will not suspect you've gone for a while…

VASILISA: And when she *does* suspect?

CAT: Well, DUH! She'll chase you! And when she's just about to catch you – chuck the towel behind you! It'll turn into a lake!

VASILISA: The *towel* will turn into a *lake*?

CAT: Well, *yes*. You stupid or something?

VASILISA: It's just that… I didn't think towels *did* that sort of thing.

CAT: You're chatting with a cat. Did you think cats did *that*? Just trust the towel!

VASILISA: Okay. So when Baba Yaga gets round the lake… what then?

CAT: Well, DUH! You chuck the hairbrush behind you!

VASILISA: And it turns into…?

CAT: Lots of trees, thicky!

VASILISA: You're sure you're not just having a joke…?

CAT: Chatty cat? Chicken-legged hut? Steely-teethed witch…?

VASILISA: Okay, I get it.

CAT: Well, *go*, then! Hell's bells! The things I'll do for a lump of cheese…

The cat spun away, so that by the click-clicking of the spinning-wheel Baba Yaga'd think the girl was still around. And Vasilisa grabbed the brush and towel, and fled.

The dog outside sprang snarling at Vasilisa. Then he stopped and licked her, remembering the crusts she'd given him. Outside the gate, the birch tree started to hit Vasilisa with its branches to obstruct her. But then the girl hung her ribbon on a branch. Whereupon the birch tree stopped hitting, and started gazing smugly at this lovely trimming.

Vasilisa ran and ran as she'd never run before. And then Baba Yaga came to the porch to sneer at her victim…

'YOU! Vile puss! Why did you betray me?' she yelled, seeing the cat at the spinning-wheel (and the spinning in a complete mess).

'When did *you* ever give me cheese?' shrugged the cat.

Baba Yaga turned on the dog. 'And *you*! Why didn't you grab the wench?'

'Nice girl! Nice crusts!' barked the dog.

'Well, why didn't YOU snitch on that child?' Baba Yaga snapped at her slave-girl.

'Cos she gave me a nice hanky... while you never gave me so much as a rag!' said the slave-girl, bravely.

'Grrrrrr! And I can't even trust my gate to grate...'

'Well, what can I do if she gives me much-needed lard?' said the gate.

'*And* my birch tree –'

'I'm not snitching! See the lovely ribbon that she

hung on my branch!'

And as she set off to chase Vasilisa, Baba Yaga vowed they'd pay… and pay, and pay…

* * * * *

Peeping back as she ran, Vasilisa spotted the flying witch… and chucked down the towel. Just as the cat had said, it became a lake… an enchanted lake that stopped Baba Yaga in her tracks. So she stormed back to her hut, spitting mad. She rounded up all her cows, and drove them back to the lake. 'Drink! DRINK!' she screeched, and drink they did… until the lake was dry.

Flying on, Baba Yaga was filled with glee as she spotted the frantic girl still fleeing. Until Vasilisa chucked the hairbrush behind her, and up sprang thousands of tall green trees. It'd take a lifetime to hack past them. So, grinding her steel teeth till they broke, Baba Yaga stormed off home… to find that cat, dog, slave-girl and all had fled…

Vasilisa made it back home at long last, trembling

all over. 'I'm back!' she called.

What massive powers does the girl possess, to have overcome the supreme Baba Yaga herself…?

Better not hang around to find out! So the step-ma fled into the forest, never to return.

And Vasilisa lived on, happy with her father. And got six black cats, just in case she ever needed more advice…

Queen of the Sun and Stars

'Queen of the Sun and Stars' based on the Russian folk tale 'The Golden Fish'.

Introducing:

Grapheme 'qu', sounds /kw/ (*queen, quantum, quack…*)

Queen of the Sun and Stars

~

Quack quack quack!

From sun-up to sun-down she never shut up.

But old Anton just went on patching his nets and catching his fish. And saying nothing to upset his wife… saying nothing, in fact.

For longer than they liked to say, Anton and Galina had lived in a shack by the lake. Time had not quenched the bitterness Galina felt for life and, above all, for her husband. And Anton had just got used to the fact that he'd made a mistake on his wedding day. A BIG mistake.

But there was no escape from wedlock this side of the grave. So Galina quacked, and spat, and glared.

And Anton fished, and fished, and fished. Seldom did they go hungry. But seldom did Anton snare extra fish to sell or barter for small comforts or tasty snacks. So day in, day out, it was fish, fish, and more smelly fish in that shack.

Then the time came when Anton pulled up his net after a day's useless fishing in the lake. So hard it was to lift that he felt sure of a massive catch. Yet there was just a lone fish squirming in the net: a fish of gold such as no man had ever seen before.

'Old man!' said the fish, as Anton gaped in shock, 'Spare me! Chuck me back into the lake and some day I may be of use to you!'

'A *golden* fish!' gasped Anton.

'Yes! And a fish you will kill unless you chuck me back! *Quickly*!' quivered the fish.

'A *fish* with *speech*!' gulped Anton.

'Yup, that's me! A golden, chatting, *quantum* fish that's – hello! – just about to run out of puff if you don't –'

'Ah! Yes! So sorry! Back you go!' responded Anton, as he chucked the fish back into the lake.

And then the golden, quantum fish turned round, gazing and grinning up at him. 'You have given me back my life. I am glad to grant you a wish in return!'

'A… *wish?*' asked the old fisherman, blankly.

'Yup! A wish! And regardless of quality or quantity, you shall have it!'

'Gosh! A wish! Well… truth to tell… I can't think of a thing,' said Anton, kicking himself at this lost chance.

'Never mind! If something springs to mind, just come and ask for it,' said the fish kindly. And he turned and dived down, down, into the lake with a loud splash.

'Well! This is an odd day, and no mistake,' said Anton to himself, as he turned for home.

'What!' quizzed Galina, when he got back to the shack empty-handed. 'Where's my fish? What's the *matter* with you, you worthless old man?'

Quaking a bit, her husband defended himself. 'I did catch a fish! A golden, quantum fish that spoke! *And* asked me to name a wish! Any wish!'

'So what did you wish for? Hand it over quick, whatever it is!'

'I… um… well… that is to say… I didn't… quite… think of a wish,' admitted Anton, by now quaking *and* quivering.

'You… *what*!' screeched Galina.

'I'm sorry!' sobbed Anton.

'Well, hell's bells! Get back to that stupid fish and tell it I want my dinner!' she yelled.

'Yes, wife!' yelped Anton, and fled back to the lake.

Where the fish quickly popped up, and asked what he wanted.

'Some dinner'd be nice, if you'd be so kind,' said the fisherman, politely.

'Go home,' said the fish, before diving back into the lake.

Sadly, the old man dragged himself home… only to find a vast dinner, the like of which he had never seen before. Plates and platters of rich fare covered every surface in his shack. Sweet-and-sour pork with mounds of rice… vast beef burgers… chicken broth… bacon sandwiches… piles of ripe grapes, melons and bananas… cakes and sweets… smelly cheeses… red wine and brown ale to wash it all down… And nothing fishy to be seen!

'Not bad,' even Galina had to admit, as she stuffed her face until she almost burst.

* * * * *

'But,' snapped Anton's wife as she kicked him

awake later, 'if the fish can do this for us, it can do a lot more. I want something *big* in place of this squalor… a proper stone house, not this shabby, down-and-out mud shack!'

'Perhaps the fish may see that as a bit… greedy?' quavered Anton.

'How dare you call me greedy!' howled Galina. 'Is a proper house so much to ask for? Did you not save that *thing's* life? And have I not put up with you for a lifetime, gods help me –'

'Yes, yes!' the hen-pecked Anton assured her, quickly. And off he went the next morning to the lake, to bow before the fish and request a big stone house.

'Go home,' was all the fish said.

And so he did. But what a home! Never had Anton seen such a house! For the first time, his wife was quivering with happiness rather than anger. She ran from the porch to the lavish kitchen and up and down the steps – *steps*! – to the sleeping quarters.

'We are indeed blessed,' said Anton, the next day.

'Blessed?' snapped Galina. 'Bah humbug! This is big, and nice, and dry – unlike that shack! But we're still… *nothings*. Nothings with a pretty house! And think of all the extra work for me, scrubbing all this extra space! I want servants to do all my tasks for me! I want to be a *lady*!'

'Oh gods,' muttered her husband, as he dragged himself back to the lake.

'Um… Oh golden fish!' he shouted, 'So sorry to bother you – *love* the big house, thank you so much! But my wife… she wants to be… well, it's a bit silly… she has this queer wish to be some sort of lady…'

And, as ever, the fish ordered Anton to go.

* * * * *

Back home, Anton found Galina dressed in silk and lace. And smugly giving orders… to servants who ran this way and that at her command!

'Well, wife, what a turn around!' he called.

'Wife? Who do you think you are?' screeched
Galina. 'I am a lady! You are a *nothing*! Servants!
Take this man outside and give him a thrashing.'

And that's just what the servants did, dragging Anton
into the yard and hitting him until he howled.

And there in the yard he stayed, slaving away day
in, day out, far harder than he had with his fishing-
nets on the lake. And for dry crusts in place of fish.
The only comfort was that he didn't see so much of
his wife. She had servants to boss about, fine gowns
to try on, thrashings to order and dishes to scoff.
So for weeks on end she'd forget she had a husband
to torment.

But the day came at last when she sent for 'that daft
old slave mopping my yard'…

'You!' Lady Galina sniffed. 'Get to that fish and tell
it I'm sick and tired of being a lady.'

'You *are*?' asked Anton, in shock. This was the last

thing he'd expected her to say.

'Yes! What use are a stone house and some petty servants? I want to be a queen!'

'You… want… to… be… a… queen?' said Anton.

'Am I not queenly?' Galina demanded.

'Er… well… that's such a grand wish,' stammered Anton. 'We… um… may have used up our quota of wishes.'

'Well,' snarled his wife, 'You just go tell Fishy that if I don't get what I want, you're going to get a big thrashing… and so is he.'

Anton quaked, and backed out, bowing. To the lake he dragged himself, tut-tutting at what the fish'd think… or say… or do. And at what kind of queen his old woman'd make.

'Oh Fish,' he began when the golden fish popped up quick as ever. 'I blush to request such a thing, but that wife of mine was a bit… insistent… that she'd like to be… er… a queen.'

'Go home,' said the fish. Anton had the queer feeling that the lake was… *darker* than before. And its waves stronger, lapping at the shore more wildly…

* * * * *

Home Anton went, if 'home' it still was. There was a vast golden palace. There was an army, standing and cheering its Queen. Servants and slaves rushed around. Hundreds of drummers and trumpet-players made a din.

And at the hub of all this fuss was Galina, in a tall golden crown and a crimson velvet gown. Lapping up the power and the glory as if she'd been born to it… with just the hint of a smirk.

The fisherman hunched up in case she spotted him, and made his way to a shed in the lavish palace gardens. There he lived while Queen Galina ruled her kingdom, with much screeching and stamping of feet and lopping off of necks.

Months passed. And the time came when being queen no longer seemed quite so much fun…

'Fetch me that old beggar I kindly allow to lurk in my grounds,' the Queen snapped to a servant.

'That fish conned me!' Anton's wife growled at him. 'Queen of a kingdom? Pah! I wish to be Queen of the Sun and Stars! Tell that to the fish or I'll feed you to the dogs!'

'Whatever,' said the fed-up Anton. As he arrived, the lake was churning blackly under a dull sky.

'What – is – it – *now*?' asked the fed-up fish, thrashing around in the waves.

'Oh, just the sun and stars – that's all!' shrugged Anton. Without a sound, the fish turned and dived back under the wild waves. And Anton just tramped home.

Home to a small shack… and a small scowling wife in a ragged black dress…

* * * * *

For all the days of his life, Anton went on casting his nets into the lake, catching plenty of fish of all shades… but never did he net a fish of gold.

Or if he did, he 'forgot' to tell his wife…

PLAY 2

King Lear:
Sharper Than Serpents' Teeth

'King Lear' based on the play by William Shakespeare.

Introducing:

Grapheme 'ea', sound /ee/ (_rea_son, h_ea_ve, pl_ea_se…)

Grapheme 'ea', sound /e/ (h_ea_d, d_ea_d, h_ea_vens…)

Grapheme 'ea' sound /ae/ (gr_ea_t, br_ea_k)

Grapheme 'ear', sound /er/ (_ear_l, _ear_ldom)

Grapheme 'ear', sound /ar/ (h_ear_t, h_ear_tless)

Grapheme 'ear', sound /ear/ (f_ear_, d_ear_, y_ear_…)

Grapheme 'ear', sound /air/ (b_ear_)

First Act:
Sharper Than Serpents' Teeth

~

CAST:

LEAR, the old King, about to give up his crown to his girls:

GONERIL, his first-born

REGAN, his second-born

CORDELIA, his third-born

DUKE OF ALBANY, husband to GONERIL

DUKE OF CORNWALL, husband to REGAN

KING OF FRANCE, wishes to wed CORDELIA

EARL OF KENT, LEAR's best chum

EARL OF GLOS, well-meaning lord. His sons:

EDGAR, his first-born

EDMUND, his bastard child

JESTER, LEAR's clown

AT KING LEAR'S PALACE:

LEAR: I am heading for my grave! And I wish to shake all cares from my elderly bones. So I am laying down my crown and dividing my kingdom between my three lucky girls! Speak up… who loves daddy best?

GONERIL: Me, me!

REGAN: No, me! With all my heart!

GONERIL: More than freedom itself; beyond all that's rich and rare; no less than life itself; as much as child ever loved –

REGAN: Yes, all that! But even more so! NOTHING makes me happy but my dad!

CORDELIA: Don't you both have husbands?

GONERIL and REGAN [*shrugging*]: Yes, what about them?

LEAR: My dear, dear girls! Here, have a third of my kingdom each! Now, Cordelia my sweet… what can you say to win even more lands than Goneril and Regan?

CORDELIA: Nothing.

LEAR [*scowling*]: Nothing will come of nothing: speak up!

CORDELIA: Unhappy as I am, I cannot heave my heart into my mouth. I'm fond of you, but you can't have all my love, I'm saving much of it for when I get wed.

LEAR: Better you had not been born than not to have pleased me better. OUT!

EARL OF KENT: My King! Check this evil rashness!

LEAR: Come not between the dragon and his fury! I loved her best! And she kicked me in the teeth! She's no lass of mine! OUT! Both of you!

KENT: Lear, please. We've been comrades for years. I don't want to abandon you with those heartless girls, just when you're getting old –

LEAR: Out! Now! Or – chop, chop – head on the block! Okay, you – French King! You still want to marry this wench, now she has nothing but my hate? She had the cheek to say she'd love her husband as much as me!

KING OF FRANCE: I think I can live with that. Yes, I'll snatch up what's cast away! Come, Cordelia, Queen of France!

LEAR: Goneril – Regan – now you'll get fifty per cent of my kingdom each! And I'll take it in turns to stay with each of you – just me and the hundred men I'm going to keep for myself!

GONERIL and REGAN: Lovely, daddy! [*Hushed*] Gods, just how senile *is* he?

AT THE EARL OF GLOS'S PALACE:

EDMUND: My father is the Earl of Glos himself! Yet I am nothing! Branded as 'base' – just cos mother wasn't wed to him! Am I not as fine, as well-made, as my brother Edgar? What's so great about dull, stale wedlock? Now gods, stand up for bastards! Aaaah! I mean hello, father!

EARL OF GLOS: What's that letter you're hiding?

EDMUND: Letter, what letter… oh heck! You got me. Okay, it's from my big brother Edgar… I'm hoping it's all a big joke.

GLOS: Why?

EDMUND: Cos it recommends that we kill you off and divide the earldom between us.

GLOS: It *what*! He cannot be such a monster! To his father, who so tenderly loves him!

EDMUND: Quite. Tell you what, I'll have a chat with him… see what's going on… [*yells*] Hey,

Edgar! Father's taken a dislike to you all of a sudden! I'd get out of here if I were you... quickly!

EDGAR [*entering*]: But... why? What have I *done*...? Some evil-doer must be lying about me!

EDMUND [*tut-tuts sadly*]: That is indeed my fear. Quick, I hear father! Flee while you still can! He wants you arrested, so I must pretend to wave my dagger at you... you do the same to me... and *flee*! *Now*!

EDGAR flees. EDMUND cuts himself with his dagger.

EDMUND: Oh father! Did you *see* that? Edgar wanted to kill me! My dear brother!

GLOS: He's no son of mine! I'll kill him! All my lands will go to you! Oh, my old heart is cracked, it's cracked!

EDMUND [*to himself*]: Tee hee! My witless kin trust me so much! Let me, if not by birth, inherit lands by my wits!

* * * * *

AT THE PALACE OF GONERIL'S HUSBAND, THE DUKE OF ALBANY:

GONERIL: Each day that maddening old man upsets me more! I'll not put up with it! It's nag, nag, nag from him, and nothing but stress from the hundred men he's inflicted on us! Which bit of 'I'm giving up my powers' did he somehow not understand? Let's try neglecting him! If he dislikes it, let him storm off to my sister, whose mind is the same as mine on this matter!

The exiled EARL OF KENT enters, in a fake beard.

KENT: Now, banished Kent, if nobody spots that the bearded bloke is you, you can help Lear... who you love however senile he's become. Oh, hello, my King! I'm here to serve you!

LEAR: You are? That's nice. I have felt a neglect of late, a lack of kindness. I dismissed it as a silly fancy, but we'll see... Ah, here's my jester!

JESTER: Ah, here's the ninny who gave away his

crown and all his lands! Nothing will come of nothing; remind me what you have now…

LEAR: Have a care, you lying scoundrel! I'll have you whipped!

JESTER: I marvel that you, Goneril and Regan are related; they'll have me whipped for telling the truth, you'll have me whipped for lying. And sometimes I am whipped for holding my peace.

GONERIL enters, frowning.

LEAR: My lass! How come you frown so?

JESTER: How happy the days when you didn't have to care if she was frowning!

GONERIL [*glaring*]: This jester – and all the other men you've inflicted on me – are nothing but pests. Don't think I'll let them get away with it! Start sacking them – NOW!

LEAR: Are – you – my – child? I cannot be awake… I cannot be Lear… Who'd speak so to the King?

Who am I? Who told me I had children? You, girl!
What name shall I call you by?

GONERIL: Oh, these silly jokes... exactly what has
to stop! You are old; so be wise. That escort brings
nothing but greed, lust, and anger. So just sack...
say... fifty of them.

LEAR: Darkness and devils! Call my men together;
get my horses! I'll not stay to vex you! I have still a
lass to welcome me! Oh hard-hearted offspring! Oh
Lear, Lear, Lear! [*Strikes his head*] Beat at this gate,
that let such folly in! Oh you gods – if Goneril
breeds, let it be a torment to her! So that she feels
how sharper than serpents' teeth it is to have a
thankless child! Oh, let me not be mad, not mad!
Sweet heaven, keep me in temper; I'd not be mad!

*LEAR reaches the EARL OF GLOS's palace, where REGAN
and her husband the DUKE OF CORNWALL are staying:*

LEAR: Will not speak with me? They are sick? They
are weary? No they are NOT!

GLOS: I am so sorry, my lord. I wish all was well between you, but…

LEAR: The King will speak with the Duke of Cornwall and his wife! I will speak to my girl! NOW!

REGAN [*enters, gritting her teeth*]: Hello father, I'm glad to see you.

LEAR: I HOPE you're glad to see me… if not, you are no lass of mine.

REGAN: Charming.

LEAR: Oh Regan, Goneril is nothing; she has treated me with such sharp-fanged unkindness –

REGAN: Surely not – it's much more likely that *you* have mistreated *her*! I keep getting letters from her about those hundred men you insist on keeping. Why don't you just beg her forgiveness?

LEAR: Over my dead body!

REGAN: Oh, I think I can hear Goneril coming

now; do bear in mind you're old and weak, and start acting like it! Sack fifty of those men and return home with her!

LEAR: Return with *her* and but fifty men? I'd rather live outside as comrade to the wolf and the owl; I'd rather grovel to that French King who wed Cordelia; I'd rather be a slave!

GONERIL [*entering*]: Fine by me. Hello, father!

LEAR: I beg you, do not make me mad; I'll not pester you. Farewell, my child; we'll no more meet. I'll not call on the gods to strike you down; I'll just stay with Regan, I and my hundred men.

REGAN: Ah... um... well... I'm not really ready for you yet... if you DO stay with me, I can't cope with more than twenty-five men.

LEAR: I gave you all —

REGAN: You made us hang around for a heck of a long time first.

LEAR: Fine! I'll go with Goneril. She offers me fifty men; you offer me twenty-five; she loves me *twice* as much as you do!

GONERIL: Think about it. I have plenty of servants to tend to you – what need you of twenty-five, ten, or even *five* men?

REGAN: Five? Hell's bells, what need have you of even a lone man?

LEAR: Oh, stop! The basest beggar has something more than he needs! Oh heavens – you see me here, a luckless old man, so full of distress! If it is you gods who stir these girls' hearts to hate me, at least do not let me bear it tamely! You vile hags! I will have such repayment on you that all the lands shall – I will do such things – what they are I cannot yet think, but they shall be *terrors*! You think I'll weep; no, I'll not weep. Storm and tempest! I have reason to weep, but this heart shall break into a hundred fragments before I'll weep!

LEAR storms out into the storm.

— End of First Act —

King Lear: As a Fly to a Wanton Lad

'King Lear' based on the play by William
Shakespeare.

Introducing:

Grapheme 'oo', sound /oo/ (s*oo*n, c*oo*t, c*oo*l...)
Grapheme 'oo', sound /oo/ (t*oo*k, l*oo*k, g*oo*d...)
Grapheme 'oo', sound /u/ (bl*oo*d, bl*oo*dy)
Grapheme 'oor', sound /or/ (p*oor*)

Second Act:
As a Fly to a Wanton Lad

~

CAST:

LEAR, the ex-King, who divided his kingdom between his lying girls, who have now chucked him out into the storm:

GONERIL, his vile first-born

REGAN, his vile second-born

CORDELIA, his third-born, exiled for refusing to tell LEAR she loved him in order to get lands

DUKE OF ALBANY, husband to GONERIL

DUKE OF CORNWALL, husband to REGAN

KING OF FRANCE, husband to CORDELIA

EARL OF KENT, LEAR's best chum, pretending to be a servant after LEAR exiled him for defending CORDELIA

EARL OF GLOS, well-meaning lord. His sons:

EDGAR, his first-born, on the run thanks to his lying brother

EDMUND, his bastard-born, plotting to be Earl, if not King

Several SERVANTS

AT THE PALACE OF THE KING OF FRANCE:

CORDELIA: Husband! I have letters from the Earls of Kent and Glos, saying my father is being ill-treated by my sisters! Quick, give me an army so I can go and save him!

KING OF FRANCE: That'd be the father who said he wished you'd never been born...?

CORDELIA: Yes. Is there a problem?

KING OF FRANCE: Er... no, my dear. By all means start a bloody conflict over that old coot. Good luck! Come home soon!

AT THE PALACE OF THE EARL OF GLOS:

EARL OF GLOS: Alas! Poor King Lear, chucked out into a howling gale by the ungrateful brats who took his kingdom!

GONERIL: Look, he was asking for it! And if he gets a bit wet it'll teach him not to go storming off like that – all Regan and I did was tell him to sack those dreadful men of his! Now shut up, or I'll *kill* you!

GLOS [*to his lad EDMUND*]: Did you hear that? We must protect the King from his girls – I'll go after him. Oh, and look at this letter from Cordelia, she's on her way with an army! Whatever you do don't tell Goneril, Regan, or those dukes they wed –

EDMUND: The secret is safe with me! [*to REGAN's husband*] Hey, you – Cornwall! Just look at this letter from Cordelia – her Frenchmen are going to attack us! And alas! My father is helping them – TREASON!

DUKE OF CORNWALL: My poor Edmund! How good you are, to put the needs of the kingdom before a son's love for his father! Regan and I will hunt him down – and you must become Earl in his place!

EDMUND: Cool! Er, I mean boo hoo, so sad about dear father...

OUT IN THE STORM:

LEAR: Let the Earth fall into the sea! Let all things

end! Winds, crack thy cheeks! All-shaking thunder, strike flat the round Earth!

EARL OF KENT: Please, go back and beg Goneril and Regan's blessing. Here's a stormy darkness that has no pity for wise men or fools.

LEAR: Gods! Let fall thy horrid elements! Here I stand, a poor, infirm, weak old man! Oh, Regan, Goneril! An old, kind father, whose frank heart gave you all – oh, that way comes madness, let me shun that… No, let a hundred imps with red burning spits come hissing in upon them!

GLOS [*entering*]: The King's wits are crazed… and mine are too. No father loved his son dearer than I my Edgar; yet now he's on the run after plotting to kill me!

KENT: Kids, eh? Look, I'll get Lear to Cordelia… you go on ahead…

LEAR: Goneril kicked the poor King her father! And as for Regan – chop her up! See what breeds in her heart!

GLOS is grabbed by REGAN and her husband the DUKE OF CORNWALL:

GLOS: Stop plucking my beard!

REGAN: Okay. We'll blind you instead. Out, vile jelly!

GLOS: OW! Where's my lad Edmund? He'll make you quit this horrid act – OW!

CORNWALL: Ha! You call upon him that hates you! It was Edmund who told us you betrayed us!

GLOS: Oh my folly! Kind gods, forgive me for trusting Edmund and betraying my good son Edgar!

SERVANT: Please, my lord of Cornwall, let the old man be!

CORNWALL: No way!

Combat starts; the DUKE OF CORNWALL and the SERVANT slay each other.

REGAN: Oh well, I suppose I'll need another husband. I must tell Edmund the glad tidings! Chuck this blind doomed old man on the dung-heap!

GLOS: As a fly to a wanton lad are we to the gods; they kill us for sport.

Exit REGAN. Enter GLOS's exiled son EDGAR, pretending to be a mad tramp:

EDGAR: What in the world has happened to father's face! Oh my gods, they've – urg! Let me help you, poor blind sir! I'm, er, Mad Tom!

AT GONERIL AND EDMUND'S CAMP:

GONERIL: Where is my husband? Why hasn't he come to meet me yet? We must stand together to defeat the French army...

SERVANT: He's on his way. But... he *smiled* when he heard that Cordelia had invaded! *And snorted* when I spoke of Glos's treason!

GONERIL: Oh, that fool! I'll deal with him! Edmund, you go and find my sister and her duke – but first kiss me! Before long I may need another husband... Hint, hint...

Exit EDMUND. Enter the DUKE OF ALBANY.

ALBANY: Oh wife, what have you done? A kingly father have you maddened! Let the heavens send down spirits to tame these vile crimes, lest humanity prey on itself, like the monsters of the deep! You... you... deformed devil! If my hands obeyed my blood, they'd tear you, flesh and bones!

GONERIL: Oh, just hush up, you lily-livered fop.

REGAN waylays GONERIL's SERVANT:

REGAN: What's my sister doing sending letters to Edmund? I'm sure that Goneril loves her husband not... and lately I spotted her giving most ardent looks to dearest Edmund! So let's get this clear: he'll be wedding ME, not her!

* * * * *

AT CORDELIA'S CAMP:

KENT: So... how did the Queen take my letter about her father?

SERVANT: Now and then a tear trilled down her delicate cheek... now and then a smile played about her ripe lips... now and –

KENT: Oh, forget it. What a pity that Lear flees from her... thanks to his burning shame at exiling her.

LEAR: When we are born we cry at entering this world of fools. I will perish bravely, like a smug bridegroom. I am every inch a King. When I do stare, see how my subjects quake!

LEAR runs away on seeing CORDELIA.

CORDELIA: Alas for my poor father! As mad as the vexed sea, singing aloud... Crowned with burdock and hemlock... Look after him lest his fury destroy him!

EDGAR is helping his blinded dad the EARL OF GLOS when they bump into GONERIL's SERVANT:

SERVANT: Ooh, goody, it's blind Glos! Queen Goneril will give me much loot for ending that worthless coot's life!

GLOS: Go ahead – you think I want to go on living?

EDGAR: Don't even THINK about it!

Combat starts; EDGAR slays the SERVANT.

SERVANT: Oh untimely death, death!

EDGAR: Hey, look, he had a letter… 'Dearest Edmund, please kill my husband Albany so we can get hitched… Much love, Goneril'! Well! Better tell poor doomed Albany…

AT CORDELIA'S CAMP:

CORDELIA: Dear father is asleep at last! Oh you kind gods! Cure the great breach in this abused

King's spirit! Is this a face to be chucked out into a gale? During that storm I'd have welcomed my enemy's dog by my fire, even if he'd bitten me! It is a wonder that both the King's wits and his life did not end!

LEAR [*wakes*]: I am a foolish, fond old man... I fear I am not in my perfect mind... Are you my Cordelia? You must bear with me. Pray you now, forget and forgive...

SERVANT: Queen Cordelia! A great host of men is coming!

REGAN and EDMUND march with an army:

REGAN: Now, sweet lord, tell me the truth: are you my sister's lover?

EDMUND: Um... er... no! No, really!

The army of GONERIL and her husband ALBANY arrive:

ALBANY: Now, I want to make it quite clear: I'm

here to stop a French army jack-booting all over this kingdom! *Not* to oppose its leader, Cordelia, or her father Lear, both of whom I admire far more than you lot, who frankly disgust me.

GONERIL and REGAN: Oh, give it a rest, you cream-faced loon.

EDMUND [*to himself*]: To both these sisters have I vowed my love! Which of them shall I take?

The army of GONERIL, REGAN, EDMUND and ALBANY clashes with the French army of CORDELIA and LEAR:

EDGAR: Hell's bells! King Lear has lost, he and Cordelia are taken!

CORDELIA: For you, oppressed King, I am cast down!

LEAR: What a hoot! Let's away to a cell and sing like captive birds! We'll live and pray and tell old tales and none shall part us!

EDMUND: Take them away! [*to his SERVANT*] And kill them!

REGAN: Woo hoo! We did it! Now Edmund and I will be wed! Ow! Why do I feel so sick?

ALBANY: Alas, you can't marry Edmund – he's vowed to my wife! Yes [*waves* GONERIL's *please-kill-my-husband letter in her face*], Edgar gave me this!

GONERIL: Oops.

EDGAR [*entering*]: I'll kill you, brother! Father is DEAD, thanks to you! When I told him who I was, between bliss and sadness his poor heart burst smilingly!

EDMUND: Try keeping silent next time, then!

They clash; EDGAR *slays* EDMUND. *A* SERVANT *rushes in.*

SERVANT: The sister-queens are dead! When Edmund fell, Goneril confessed to putting venom in Regan's drink... and then stabbed herself!

ALBANY: Well, at least Cordelia's okay –

LEAR *enters, carrying* CORDELIA's *body.*

LEAR: Howl, howl, howl! Oh, you are men of stone. I killed the slave that was a-hanging her... but she's dead as earth!

EDGAR: Thy older girls too are dead.

LEAR: No, no, no life! Why no breath at all for Cordelia when a dog, a horse, a rat, has life? Oh, you will come no more; never, never, never, never, never. Oh – do you see this? Look on her: look, her lips! Look there, look there! Cordelia breathes! Ha! This redeems all the agony that ever I felt –

LEAR keels over.

KENT [*entering*]: She breathes...?

ALBANY: Sorry... dead as a dodo. Like her father.

KENT: All's cheerless, dark and deadly! Break heart, I prithee, break!

EDGAR: Yeah...that Shakespeare bloke – *not* in a good mood...

Puss in Boots

'Puss in Boots' based on the French fairy tale by Charles Perrault.

Introducing:

Grapheme 'ow', sound /oe/ (*sorr<u>ow</u>ful, pill<u>ow</u>, <u>Ow</u>en*...)

Words that may not be wholly decodable at this stage:

y our(s)

Puss in Boots

~

The Miller was dying. Well, he was an old man, and he'd had a good life. A job that he liked, that had kept his family fed. A loving wife who he was keen to meet up with in heaven. And three strapping lads to stand round his death-bed looking sorrowful… and just a bit hopeful over who'd get his goods.

'Bill!' wheezed the Miller. 'As my eldest lad you will get the mill… Work hard, keep grinding that corn, and you'll be okay…'

'Thanks, dad! I will!'

'Robert… the mule is yours… let your brother borrow it to turn the mill-wheel in return for a share of the profits…'

'Sure thing, pa!'

'Owen, my last-born... you get the cat!'

'The... WHAT?' screeched Owen, so sure he'd misheard that he started sticking fingers in his ears to clear out the wax.

'The c-c-cat,' wheezed the Miller, with almost his last breath.

'The c-c-CAT?' Owen was still having problems coming to terms with what his ears seemed to be telling him.

'Yes, yes! The cat! The moggy! The feline! The black-and-silver striped animal that catches the rats! Oh, for heaven's sake... *that* cat over *there*!' And, worn out by his last words, the Miller slumped back onto his pillow, dead.

Owen looked at the cat. The cat looked at Owen.

Owen curled his lip in scorn.

So did the cat.

* * * * *

Bill liked to think of himself as tactful. As did
Robert. So they let Owen gloom around the mill
for a week following the Miller's death before they
asked him if he had 'plans'.

'No,' said Owen, truthfully.

'Well, you'd better start making some, fast,'
snapped Bill, dropping this 'tact' stuff. 'This is no
longer your home! Why don't you go and seek your
fortune or something?'

'Yeah – away with you - and take your flea-ridden
tabby with you!' added Robert.

'Yes, I'm sure Puss will come in useful for, er...
presenting you with dead birds or something,'
sniggered Bill.

So Owen packed up all his goods in a red-and-
white-spotted hanky, tucked the spitting cat under
his arm, and stormed off.

* * * * *

Owen hadn't got a hundred yards when the moggy took over.

'Well… you're in a bit of a fix, are you not?' he asked, helpfully.

'What's it to you, flea-bag?' demanded the Miller's lad.

'Let's get some things clear,' said Puss, jumping to the ground and fixing Owen with a glowing green gaze. 'I can make you rich and happy beyond your wildest dreams. But you *do as I tell you.*

'Firstly: to you, I am *Mister* Cat. Not "Hey, you!"; not "Moggy"; not "That flea-ridden fur-ball"; and not "Oochy-coochy fluffy munchkin". Okay?'

'Okay… Mister Cat!' said Owen meekly.

'Secondly, I want some boots.'

'Why?' asked Owen in surprise.

'Why? Hell's bells – why do *you* have boots?'

'Fine!' snapped Owen. 'I'll have some made for you! With the last of my cash!'

And he did. Soon Puss was strutting around in tall shiny boots looking more elegant than ever. Then he told the Miller's lad to get his clothes off and jump in the lake.

'Please tell me you're joking,' begged Owen.

'Nope,' purred Puss, sharpening his talons on the nearest tree as a hint for the brat to do just as he was told.

'But… it's so cold! There's a wind blowing! I'll be chilled to the marrow of my bones!'

'So…?' asked Puss, with a feline shrug. 'You need a bath. And you'll never catch a Princess wearing those rags.'

'Princess? WHAT Princess!' screeched the Miller's lad. He'd always been a bit slow off the mark.

Humans! Sometimes Puss wondered why he bothered.

* * * * *

Well, the Miller's lad was in the lake at last, splashing away and sobbing something about freezing to death. While Mister Cat raced from meadow to meadow, glaring, spitting, puffing up his fur and waving his talons at all the workers. 'You – WILL – tell – the – King – that – the – Duke – of – Carabas – owns – this – land!' shouted Puss, slowly and clearly. The workers quaked, and nodded frantically. And bent low to mow the grass, or sow seeds in rows, or throw stones at crows… all to grow crops for a fine harvest.

As the King rode by in his grand gig, with his sixteen-year-old lass at his side, he spotted all the workers slaving away. 'Who owns these meadows?' he asked them. As a matter of fact, they belonged to a nasty troll… but the troll was off in his palace and the cat was swishing around nearby. 'The Duke of Carabas!' shouted all the workers. The King and his lass were looking impressed, when…

'Help! Help! My [*the cat gritted his teeth*]… my *lord and master*, the Duke of Carabas, has lost all his garments while swimming in the lake! Some vile robber has made off with them!'

'No problem!' said the King, keen to assist such a rich lord, and he sent a servant back to his palace to fetch his finest garments.

With the cat hissing orders at him, Owen overcame his shock at being promoted to duke – 'UH?' Donned the splendid garments – 'For *me*?' And made quite a hit with the Princess – 'You're joking! A *Princess*!' – as they rode on together.

Meanwhile, the intrepid moggy was striding boldly up to the troll's palace.

'Good afternoon, Mister Troll,' he said politely. 'I have heard such wonderful tales of you that I had to see for myself. But surely they were lying!

You can't *really* shape-shift…?'

And, just like that, the vast ugly troll had vanished, and there stood a splendid spotted feline, all fur and fangs.

'Bravo!' clapped Puss. 'But… Oh, never mind…'

'But what?' bellowed the monster-feline.

'Oh, nothing… Nothing at all… It's just that, well, I always think *small* is best – or at least hardest – don't you…? See, even *I* can puff myself up quite big' – Puss arched his back and stood all his fur up on end – 'But I do sometimes desire to be as small as, say, a rat…'

'I can turn myself into a rat! I just don't want to! Nasty smelly vermin, they are!'

'Yes, they are,' purred Puss, in his most sarcastic tone. 'But all the humans… they just don't *get* it. They say you're just not up to shrinking to the size of a rat!'

'I'll show them!' bellowed the troll, and then and there he turned himself into a rat.

'Sucker!' hissed Puss in Boots as he opened wide his mouth and swallowed the ex-troll.

* * * * *

With purr-fect timing, the King's gig turned up at the palace gates.

'My lord King! *Hic*! My most – *burp*! – lovely Princess! A hundred welcomes to the lowly home of my… grrr… my *lord and master* the Duke of – *belch* – Carabas!'

'Who, me?' asked Owen.

'Yes, you! Get with it!' snapped the cat, still trying hard not to throw up the troll.

'All those lands… Plus this great palace…' mused the King…

'And such a lovely face… Such a shy smile…!'

gushed the Princess, who'd inherited her father's
mild tendency to dim-wittedness...

* * * * *

The Princess and the so-called Duke of Carabas
were wed within the week, with her father's
blessing. They gave each other much happiness.

But for the cat life wasn't quite so wonderful. Sure,
he was *Lord* Puss, had endless troll-sized bowls of
cream, and ten sets of shining boots... but for some
reason the fun of consuming rats had utterly
vanished...

Blowing in the Wind

'Blowing in the Wind' based on the Indian folk tale 'Shiva and Bhasmasura'.

Consolidation of letter/sound correspondences introduced.

Blowing in the Wind

~

There were lots of things Basmas didn't like. In fact – being a vile demon – Basmas was sometimes hard-pressed to name a lone thing that he *did* like. But it was only when he heard the tale of the Hermit that he decided to do something about his all-consuming hatred.

The Hermit had prayed so long and so hard that the great god Shiva himself had appeared, and granted him the wish of his heart. So Basmas sat on a hill-top and prayed to Shiva, year after year, until swallows nested in his beard and moss crept over his feet.

* * * * *

Impressed, Shiva turned up and offered this seemingly-devoted man a wish.

'Not before time!' Basmas muttered to himself.

'No, no, lord!' protested Basmas to the god, with a sarcastic smile. 'Your blessing is all I've ever desired!'

'But you must desire something else!' insisted Shiva, unwisely.

'Oh, if you insist – let each person I tap with my left hand turn to ashes!'

'ASHES?' screeched Shiva. 'Are you quite sure you don't want to turn them into, um, crows or something?'

'Nope... ashes... I wanna see them blowing in the wind,' said the demon smugly, well aware that the god must keep his word. Whatever the cost.

'Granted,' said Shiva, with a heavy heart.

* * * * *

'Thanks, pal! Mind if I test out my thrilling gift...

ON YOU!' bellowed Basmas, leaping forward. Shiva turned and fled, with the demon following fast behind him, waving his left hand and cackling like a madman.

'Need a hand?' asked the god Vishnu, spotting the race with some surprise.

'Hell's bells! YES!' panted Shiva, diving into the nearest hole.

Moments later, the bellowing demon was shocked to see a glowing woman in a yellow sari standing in his path.

'You! Tell me where that Shiva is or I'll – ooh! You're so lovely! I must have you for my wife!' gasped Basmas.

'Alas! I have sworn to wed no man… unless he were to match me in the Dance!' said Vishnu, in her female form.

'I can dance!' said the demon eagerly. 'Show me the steps and I'll match them!'

* * * * *

So Vishnu was dancing... and prancing... and skipping... with her yellow sari swirling around her. And – more slowly – Basmas capered and twirled, nearly tripping over his big feet. On and on it went, day after day, the demon always a step behind, the hill-top shaking below them...

... Until the moment when Vishnu sank, oh so gracefully, to the ground with her hands on her head.

'About time!' bellowed the sore-footed demon as he too sank – less gracefully – to the ground. He placed his hands on his head...

... And exploded into a heap of ashes...

The Stars of Orion

'The Stars of Orion' based on Roman myths of Diana and Orion.

Introducing:

Grapheme 'ai', sound /ae/ (_b<u>ai</u>t_, _disd<u>ai</u>n_, _afr<u>ai</u>d..._)

Words that may not be wholly decodable at this stage:

g oe s

Note: Bacchus

The Stars of Orion

~

Who hasn't had an off-day? Who hasn't got a bit
cross at times? Who hasn't fixed a problem in a way
that they *may*, after carefully thinking it over,
suspect wasn't so fantastic after all? Who hasn't
tricked an irritating sister into killing her lover –
oh, that's just me, then?

* * * * *

Hi – Apollo here. Yup, *that* Apollo. God of the
Sun.

Yeah, the Sun… big round glowing ball thing in
the sky… gives you all that heat and stuff…?

Not that I get much *thanks* for it… sure, now and
then a fellow may sacrifice a sick hen or something
in gratitude for stopping the Earth being cold and
dark and *dead* and suchlike…

But, sad to say, most of the acclaim goes to dad. Just cos he's King of the Gods and chucks thunderbolts around. And I'm afraid there's plenty of acclaim left over for my twin Diana, Goddess of Hunting and the Moon. You'd not think there'd be such a *fuss* over something as useless as that old Moon, but it's all 'Just see what she does to the tides!' and 'Oh, what shining silver loveliness!' from the humans. And, over and over from my fellow gods… 'Apollo, why can't you stop chasing all the girls and be more like your sister – she's just so *pure?*'

Pah!

If Diana wants to spend all her time making seas bob up and down, and killing small helpless animals, that's her problem. It's not some sort of *morality* – just try asking those small helpless animals. Oh! You *can't*! What with them being DEAD!

Besides, Diana dropped the 'Oh, look at me, I'm just so pure. And shiny!' stuff the second she spotted Orion…

* * * * *

Yup, *that* Orion. Sure, he makes a pretty set of stars
(so really, I don't see what all the *fuss* is about) but
as a mortal he was just a big ugly lumbering hunter.
Can't *think* what Diana was so wild about. Instead
of reacting normally – say, a merry hunt up hill and
down dale, ending with an arrow in Orion's heart
and a cry of 'Tally-ho!' – she started *blushing* at
him. (The Moon turned a really silly shade of
pink.) And *cooing*. And fluttering her lashes.

* * * * *

When I complained, Diana said that she and Orion
were Just Good Chums. That she'd *finally* met a
man who was nearly as good a hunter as she, so
she'd jolly well hunt alongside him if she wanted.
Even if he *was* a mere mortal. She may also have
accused me of *envy*. (Ha! In your *dreams*, Sister!)

So I shrugged in casual disdain, and went on my
way. Plotting how to kill Orion. I mean, I wasn't
gonna have my sister mess around with a mortal,
was I! Okay, so the rest of us gods do (all the time),

but at least we tend to go for *lookers*. Have I said how *big* and *ugly* this man is – er, used to be? Plus, he had a *dog*. I hate dogs – a bit of sunshine and they're panting away like you're *killing* them. (Cats, now – I like cats. And cats like me. They really know how to *bask* in the Sun, those fellas.)

Well, I waited. And waited. My family always think I'm hot-tempered just cos I'm, well, hot. But you don't drive a dirty great ball of fire across the sky every day for eternity without learning a *bit* of self-control.

* * * * *

So it was weeks later I met my sister for a bit of a chat. I asked after her hulking great man. I even asked after his dog! Then… just in passing… I slipped in the bait: a remark about a big contest dad was thinking of holding. A bunch of sporting events for all of us gods.

'I'll obtain *all* the prizes,' I bragged.

'Maybe you will,' said Diana, tossing back her

silvery mane with that irritating silvery titter of hers. 'All but the archery.'

'So you think small Cupid will gain the archery prize?' I asked, laying on the thickness a bit, well, thick.

'*That* fat kid – as *if*! Am *I* not the greatest archer on Earth or in Heaven?' asked my vain twin, swallowing the bait.

'Nope, don't think so!' I said, in my sunny way.

'You want to put it to the test? Fine! Name your target!'

'Ooh… how about… that log-or-whatever-it-is over *there*?' I asked, oh so casually, as I indicated a small speck far off in the sea.

It goes without saying that this speck was the head of Orion, having a nice swim. And it goes without saying that the words had barely left my lips when *whoosh*! went Diana's arrow and *splat*! went the poor fellow.

Tee hee!

Well, I clapped her fine aim and got well away from there before those stupid tides of Diana's swept the body ashore.

* * * * *

Then I laid low for a while. I have to say, the weeping and the wailing went on for a *rather* long time. As did the threats to slice me into shreds.

And I'm afraid the other gods weren't exactly... over the Moon. (Pun intended.) Luckily, dad can't be bothered with these small tiffs. But Bacchus, god of wine, refused to invite me to his revels. Mars, god of war, offered to punch me on the nose. Neptune, god of the sea, rose from the deeps to wave his trident around in a nasty manner. Oh, and Minerva the brain-box treated me to a long lecture on the subject of 'Messing Up Your Sister's Love Life – It's Just Not Healthy'.

Well, at least Venus took my side. She'd got fed up of hundreds of years of Diana telling her how 'A

Solo Life Is A Good And Happy Life' and hinting that, frankly, Venus is a bit of a harlot. (Hello! Which bit of 'Goddess of Love' was Dear Di somehow not getting?)

But hey, it's not as if even the most fed-up god was willing to *do* something really nasty to me. I'm the flaming *Sun* – vital or WHAT? *I* go out, and it's curtains for... well... *everything*.

* * * * *

So what did my sister go and do instead of ripping me to shreds...?

She stuck that good-for-nothing mortal in the sky!

She turned Orion the late lamented loser into stars and set him up there to shine in the Milky Way!

Where, each time darkness fell, Diana drove the Moon across the sky and gazed adoringly at him.

Yeah... so much for 'We're Just Good Chums', eh?

Diana even turned his flipping *dog* into stars too! Seems Sirius the faithful bootlicker was *pining* for his master (boo hoo!) and refusing to wag his silly doggy tail or something, so… lo and behold! He's in the sky as well, eternally following the moronic Orion around the Milky Way!

Get a *life*, dog!

* * * * *

I don't *do* 'regret', okay?

I don't do 'Sorry' or 'I'm so wicked' or 'Hey, maybe it's a pity I didn't let my sister get hitched to some stupid mortal'.

Or 'Gosh, poor Diana, getting an eternity of pain in return for those weeks of happiness'…

I mean, maybe they *were* Just Good Chums – in which case, what's the big deal? They get to see each other again and again – every time I leave the sky and that nasty cold darkness falls!

Or maybe not – in which case, who can blame me for a bit of payback? *Hundreds* and *hundreds* of years of smug lectures on how *pure* Diana is!

All the same… now and then… I glance up at those so-shiny (and SO irritating) stars of Orion and wonder… if a happy sister was *such* a dreadful thing to put up with…

Hell's bells! Yes it WAS!

GLOSSARY

~

APOLLO, the Sun-God; twin brother to DIANA; JUPITER'S son

BACCHUS, wild God of wine and revels; lover of VENUS

CUPID, son of VENUS and MARS; shoots golden arrows of desire

DIANA, the Moon-Goddess; huntress; twin sister to APOLLO

JUNO, Goddess for females and fertility; JUPITER'S wife

JUPITER, King of the Gods; hurler of thunderbolts

MARS, the War-God; lover of VENUS

MERCURY, messenger of the Gods

MINERVA, Goddess of wisdom, learning, arts and industry

NEPTUNE, the Sea-God; lover of VENUS

ORION, the hunter; killed and turned to stars by his beloved DIANA

PLUTO, God of the Underworld

SATURN, God of farming

SIRIUS, ORION'S dog, also turned to stars

VENUS, Goddess of love

VULCAN, God of fire; ugly blacksmith; long-suffering husband of VENUS

STORY 6

Rainbow
Snake

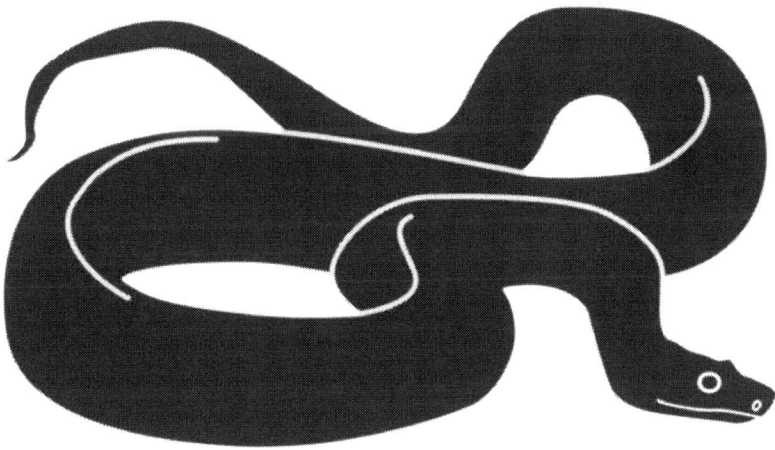

'Rainbow Snake' based on the Australian Aborigine myth.

Consolidation of letter/sound correspondences introduced.

Rainbow Snake

Forever, the Great Spirit had ruled. And forever, he had been loved by all. But now came Chinimin to rebel against the Lord of All. Chinimin dared to sneer and snigger at the Great Spirit – his *own father*.

In his fury and his fear, the Great Spirit rushed at his son. And in his fury and his fear, Chinimin dropped the sniggering and the sneering and backed away. But the Great Spirit set about beating him with a club.

Chinimin grabbed a spear and stabbed back. Pained almost unto death, the Great Spirit twisted in agony, his body curling into the shape of a vast snake…

Sobbing and hissing, the Great Spirit dragged himself into the River that split the Spirit World from the World Below. He fell into the waters…

And fell…

To the World Below.

That barren, dusty globe called Earth…

* * * * *

Crash!

Where he landed, a huge crater formed.

And filled with water from the Spirit River…

And that world which had been nothing but dust and darkness suddenly gained its very first lake.

And upon that land, from the hole torn in the sky by the Snake's fall, the sun blazed.

* * * * *

Slowly, in agony, the Snake who had been the Great

Spirit dragged himself across the dust of the world. And where he passed, the endless flatness turned to hills and hollows. And behind him flowed water from the Spirit River, to form streams and lakes upon that barren domain.

With water came life. From the dust sprang flowers of all shades, from the red of the Snake's blood to the gold of the sun.

The Snake, too, took on those glowing shades as he twisted and crept across the Earth. From his blood, and from the unfamiliar sun, and from the rain and hail that teemed from the torn sky, all the animals on Earth were formed. Among them, Man.

And, at last, the Snake's long agony ended. Gathering himself, he sprang upwards from the Earth, back to the Spirit World that was his domain. Only the rainbow of his shed skin remained, to hang in the sky... above the fresh, blazing world of life.

Anansi has Problems

'Anansi has Problems' based on the African folk tales 'How Anansi Tricked his Father', 'Fire and Anansi', 'The Yam-Hills', and 'How the World Got Wisdom'.

Introducing:

Grapheme 'ou', sound /oo/ (*soup, group, youth*...)

Grapheme 'ou', sound /u/ (*youngster, touched, famous*...)

Grapheme 'our', sound /or/ (*gourd, course, poured*...)

Grapheme 'oul', sound /oo/ (*could, would, should*)

Part 1:
Problems with Dad

Of course, Anansi didn't get on that well with his dad. Anansi was a Spider. A big, famous, cunning, back-from-the-dead kind of Spider. But... a *Spider*.

Anansi's dad was Nyame the Sky God.

You can see why Anansi felt a bit... lacking. If shrinks had existed in Africa in those days, they would have had a lovely time discussing Anansi's 'complexes'.

But Anansi didn't want to lord it over the entire world. He just wanted those *tales*.

Those amazing... astounding... fantastic... wondrous... *ultra-cool* tales that Nyame loved to make up and loved to tell to his subjects down on Earth.

And Anansi *wanted them*.

He wanted those divine tales to be *his*, in the way that all other things belonged to his father.

But however much he nagged and begged and pleaded to be given the groovy tales, the Sky God would just shake his wise head. 'Sorry, youngster – don't you touch my tales!'

Until the day came when the All-Father got so sick of his son's pestering that he said: 'Okay, youngster – pass three tests and you get all my wondrous tales, okay? Fail and of course you stop pestering me!'

'Deal!' enthused Anansi, confident that *of course* his famous cunning would win the day... even with the Sky God as his opponent.

'Great! First, you'll bring me a gourd full of wasps! Without getting stung!'

'A... gourd... full... of... wasps,' repeated Anansi slowly, hoping that he had misheard.

'That's the ticket!' said his father, cheerfully.

So Anansi gritted his teeth, and fetched himself a gourd – the dry shell of a pumpkin – and bored a hole in it. Then he had his brainwave. He sat near a group of wasps and waited for it to rain. And rain it did. Sheets and sheets of water poured from the sky. Whereupon… 'You poor wasps!' shouted Anansi. 'Of course you should fly into this gourd before you all drown! Quick!'

And in they went, wasp after wasp, until the gourd was full, and buzzing. Buzzing rather loudly and indignantly by the time the Spider presented the gourd to his dad.

'Good show, youngster!' scowled the Sky God. 'Next you can get me a tiger!'

'A… *tiger?*' howled Anansi, indignantly.

'Yup… big red-and-yellow stripy cat-thing,' said Nyame, smugly.

'A tiger! Of course! Why not!' said the Spider, sourly, and stormed off back to Earth. There, he dug a pit, covered it over with greenery, and waited for the nearest tiger to fall in.

'Why, Tiger!' Anansi shouted when a tiger had finally plummeted into the pit, 'Whatever are you doing down there?'

'Some vile beast has set a trap for me! Quick, help me out before they come and KILL me!'

'Well, of course I'd just *love* to help, but… you're so *big* and so *scary*… will you promise me your everlasting gratitude from this day forward?'

'Yes!' yelped the poor wounded Tiger. Whereupon the Spider hit him over the head with a big stick.

With help from a group of pals, Anansi dragged the sleeping Tiger off to the Sky God, who pouted and pouted… and demanded a python.

'No problem!' said Anansi, who was really getting the hang of this by now. He found the tallest of bamboo trees, cut it down, and dragged it to where a great green Python was curled up asleep.

'Oh! If only I could tell which was longer – the Python or the pole!' he shouted.

'Uh?' said the sleepy Python, uncurling himself.

'My dad – the SKY GOD – swears that no mere snake is as long as the longest bamboo tree, but I'm not so sure,' said the cunning Spider. 'In fact, we had a bit of a bet about it.'

'Of course I'm longer than a stupid bit of wood!' snapped the Python, and attempted to prove it. He touched the pole… and stretched out… and stretched out…

'Your tail is curling!' said Anansi. 'I'll just fix it to the pole with this bit of vine I happen to have…' And he did.

'Your tummy is curving!' said the Spider. 'Hold still while I just secure it with the vine… yup, that's the ticket! Come on, you can do it!'

And, while the snake was straining and stretching to his utmost, Anansi looped the vine around his head, and – hell's bells! – Python was stuck fast to the pole!

'Dad! Snake-on-a-stick! Just as requested!' shouted Anansi, dragging his thrashing, hissing victim into the sky.

And so it came to pass that, to this day, all astounding tales are called *Anansi* tales. Nyame was sad to lose his tales, but quite proud that, despite his absurd number of legs, the youngster should be such a chip off the old block.

Part 2:
Problems with Fire

Time was, Anansi and Fire were the best of chums. Every evening, Anansi would stroll over to Fire's yard with some food for Fire to kindly cook for him while they chatted.

'You should come and visit our hut some time! Let

my wife and me return your kindness! Make you
soup or something!' the Spider told Fire.

'I would if I could!' Fire said. 'But look – no legs!'

Anansi was famous for his cunning. Of course he
wasn't going to be put off by a small thing like *that*!

'If I should lay a path of dry grass from your yard
to my hut, why then, you wouldn't *need* to come by
foot! You would just burn your way along it!'

And Anansi scattered the dry grass and twigs as he
rushed home to tell his wife they would have a
visitor that evening.

'You – did – WHAT!' his wife screamed, and she
fled the hut as fast as lots of legs could carry her.

Anansi was still tut-tutting at his wife's cowardly
back when Fire blazed along the path, engulfed
his hut, and – ow *ow* OUCH! – burnt him to death.

After he came back to life, Anansi was a bit more
wary of his old chum Fire.

Part 3:
Problems with the Number Nine

~

Anansi was digging away on his nine tall hills, all chock-a-block with yams. He was tired, he was hungry, the yams were unripe, he'd always hated hard work. In short, he was in a *very* sour mood. When he suddenly remembered the witch who had declared the number nine out of bounds – utterly taboo. Of course, Anansi didn't really have much trust in spells and suchlike, but why not give it a go?

So when Mister Hog came down the path, Anansi started to sob. Being a nice fellow, Hog asked what the matter was.

'I – can't – *count!*' wailed Anansi. 'All day I've been trying to count my yam-hills, but blow me down if I can get past six!'

'Oh, no problem!' beamed helpful Mister Hog,

waving a trotter at each hill in turn and counting slowly for the poor thick Spider's benefit. 'Look – 1, 2, 3, 4, 5, 6, 7, 8… you have *nine* hills!'

And poor Mister Hog dropped down dead, then and there.

The pork was yummy.

* * * * *

The next day, it was the turn of that nice Miss Cow. She was good at maths… Anansi loved oxtail soup… the rest, as they say, is history…

* * * * *

On the third morning, Anansi was sitting on a yam-hill feeling a bit hungry when Mister Chimp passed by.

'Oh! *Sob*! My Chimp pal! Be a dear and count my hills for me – I'm – *sob* – such a nitwit I keep losing track! What you must think of me!'

'Of course!' said Chimp, so cheery. '1, 2, 3, 4, 5, 6, 7, 8 – and the hill you are sitting on!'

'You rotter! You cheat!' screeched Anansi, in a towering temper. 'That's not how you should count! It's 1, 2, 3, 4, 5, 6, 7, 8… NINE!'

And Anansi dropped dead.

He didn't try messing with Chimp much after *that*.

Part 4: Problems with Wisdom

~

Nyame the Sky God was getting mellow in his declining years.

Well… some said 'mellow'. Others said 'odd'. There were even some votes for 'stark raving bonkers'.

For what should he go and do but entrust wisdom

itself to his son the Spider! Anansi the Trickster! Our old pal with all those legs!

And not just SOME wisdom... oh no, Nyame gave *all the wisdom on Earth* to Anansi. In a POT, for heaven's sake.

Of course, 'smug' doesn't begin to cover how Spider looked that day.

But not for long...

* * * * *

It goes without saying that Anansi wasn't exactly planning to *share* his windfall with any other person or group. Nope, our charming Spider rather liked the idea of owning the planet's entire stock of wisdom while the rest of us blundered round in the dark.

The first thing oh-so-wise Anansi did was to work out how none could ever touch his pot of wisdom. He spotted the perfect hiding place – the tallest, smoothest tree in all the lands. After all, our Spider had lots more legs as well as lots more wisdom than the rest of us – he could get up there, no problem! While – tee hee! – the thick, lesser-legged masses would just be milling around at the base of the tree!

So up he went, clutching the pot with several of his legs.

And down he went, as the tree was *so* tall... and *so* smooth... and all that wisdom was *so* heavy.

Three times Anansi attempted to get up that tree, and three times Anansi came crashing down... curling into a ball around the pot of wisdom each time so it wouldn't get smashed.

* * * * *

At last the Spider's smart young son, Kuma, strolled up to see what was going on.

'Dad!' said Kuma, in the tone all youths adopt towards old parents. 'If you really want to get up there, just fix the pot to your back! All your legs'll be free to dig into the tree-bark! Easy!'

And was Anansi *happy* and *grateful* to have his problem solved…?

No way!

Of course, Anansi was hopping mad at this proof that a mere youth had some wisdom of his own. The Spider wasn't the proud owner of all the wisdom on Earth after all! So he hurled the pot to the ground and jumped up and down on it – wounding his poor feet. While howling swear-words. Loudly.

Wisdom poured out, spreading across the lands of the Earth…

We all got a bit.

Not much. But a bit.

Thanks, Anansi!

Doom of the Gods

'Doom of the Gods' based on the the Norse myths of the gods.

Introducing:

Grapheme 'ew', sound /oo/ (_new, grew, chew_...)
Grapheme 'aw', sound /or/ (_yawn, paw, jaw_...)

Words that may not be wholly decodable at this stage:

souls	eye(s)	one	once

Doom of the Gods

~

'You – did – WHAT?' howled Odin, King of the Gods, to Loki the Trickster. 'You – wed – an – *ice-troll*? What did you think you were DOING! You're a *god*! Okay, an awful, spiteful kind of god, but still, a *god*! It's against the law to get hitched to a hulking troll from a race destined to destroy us AND the world when Ragnarok comes –'

'Hey, wasn't your ex an ice-troll?' drawled Loki.

'That was *different*!' spluttered Odin. 'I'm the god of wisdom! I gave up an EYEBALL for wisdom, *if* you recall! I foresaw that it was my *destiny* to marry Jord –'

'Yeah, yeah, whatever,' sneered an unimpressed Loki. 'Anyway, what makes you think it wasn't my destiny to marry Angurboda? I really fancy her!

Plus she said she'd eat me if I didn't make her my lawful wedded wife!'

'*As I was saying,*' snarled Odin, 'Jord and I were destined to wed, and to have Thor, to be Protector of the Gods. But I have a *very* bad feeling about the sort of children you'll have by this, this Angur-thingy –'

'Not as bad a feeling as you would have if you'd met them,' said Loki, cheerily. 'Just between you and me, our Hel's not exactly a looker, Fenric totally freaks me out, and as for that scary Serpent –'

'Am I to understand,' said the King of the Gods, gritting his teeth, 'that you and your bride have already been blessed with offspring?'

Sensing a threat, the glib trickster suddenly became the doting father. 'Darling Fenric is such a big, fluffy wolf!' he gushed. 'We have a fantastic Snake who can stretch like there's no tomorrow! And as for our lass – okay, so she's part-carcass, but *aside* from the rotting bits she's really quite cute –'

'You will bring them before me,' decreed Odin. '*Now.*'

'You're not going to... *hurt* them or... anything?' Loki quavered. 'They're just small kids! Okay, quite big kids... massive, in fact, but –'

'Shut up, Loki,' said Odin, weary and bitter. 'I shall not slay these monsters. They are fate. They are the doom of the gods. We cannot, will not, shed the blood of children to try to side-step fate: the Endless Winter, the Last Combat of Ragnarok, the Earth perishing in fire and flood, the End of Days –'

'Oh well, that's okay then,' chirped Loki. 'I'll go and fetch my poppets!'

* * * * *

The gods' attitude when they saw Loki's family left something to be desired.

'Ugg! Make them go away!' squealed Sif the Golden-Haired.

'That is one dirty great snake – can I kill it?' yelled Thor the Thunderer.

'*Please* tell me you're kidding!' begged blind Hod as he was told what was padding, slithering, and stomping towards him.

'Ouch!' murmured Saga, the goddess of history, suddenly getting the feeling her subject would soon be... well... *history*.

'Welcome to Asgard!' Freya, Queen of the Gods, managed to choke out before she spewed up her breakfast.

'Yes, welcome to Asgard, dear chums!' beamed Balder the Beloved. For the first time it occurred to his family that a sunny nature could be a bit... irritating.

'We thank you!' shouted Angurboda. Her sons growled and hissed agreement. Her lass twitched decaying lips in what was almost a smile.

* * * * *

'We are here,' said Odin, suddenly old and weary with the burden of the world upon his shoulders, 'to decide the fate of these three. Spawn of the Trickster-God, they are born to be the doom of gods and men. *Put that hammer down*, Thor! They are not to be harmed! The future, once woven by the Norns, cannot be undone –'

'Yeah… sorry about that…' muttered the Norns, the three sister-goddesses who wove the Web of Time. 'But if it's any comfort, *some* of you will be reborn into the next cosmos once ours has been destroyed…'

The gods considered this promise and found it small comfort. The deathly hush was at last broken by Sif, as she tossed back her golden locks.

'Yeah, but will the next cosmos have good hair-care products?' she asked.

Every god and monster in the hall rolled its eyes.

'Er… moving on,' said Odin, 'I will grant Hel a realm of her own, to rule as she sees fit. And I will give her Garm to be her watchdog, to see that no one ever escapes her domain. A part-dead maid should rule over dead souls –'

'Hey! Those souls are ours!' called Freya, mistress of Freya's Hall, which, along with Odin's Valhalla, housed the dead.

'Indeed, the spirits of those who perish bravely in combat will remain the concern of the King and Queen of the gods,' swore Odin. 'But for those sad losers who don't, there shall be Hel's... er... *hell*. Agreed?'

'Agreed,' pouted Freya.

'Agreed – what a chance for the young lass!' said Loki and Angurboda, proudly.

'Fine by me,' shrugged Hel, maggots falling from her rotting lips.

And so it was that she and Garm the great brown dog sank down, down, to her brand-new domain, there to gather in those pitiful souls who had not perished in combat.

* * * * *

'And as for you who are the Midgard Serpent!' said Odin to the vast snake. 'Let all the seas of the world be your kingdom!'

'Hang on – those seas are *my* kingdom!' snapped Ran, goddess of storms and of perished mariners.

'Does it not seem... likely... that there'll be a LOT more dead mariners once this fellow is thrashing about under the waves?' asked Odin.

'Well, if you put it like *that*...' said Ran, slowly...

'Great! So glad we agree!' yelled Odin, as he *hurled* the Midgard Serpent into the green depths of the seas.

'Don't worry,' he assured the Serpent's shocked-looking parents, 'he'll be just fine. And he'll pop up again, come Ragnarok. More's the pity.'

'He'd BETTER – or else!' snapped Loki. 'His

mother and I are really gonna miss him… and dear Hel… so I strongly advise you don't do anything *quite* so drastic to our third child.'

'Let Fenric the Wolf remain in Asgard,' twitched Odin, nervously. 'We gods shall rear him as a son, in the hope he'll turn out to be… um… nicer than he looks.'

'Grrrrrrrrrrr!' said Fenric.

* * * * *

And so the years dragged by, heavy with doom.

Hel sniggered on her throne of bones as she watched her ever-growing number of subjects. The dead milled around, wailing with a despair that would outlast eternity. While, beneath the waves, her brother the Serpent grew… and grew… until he stretched all the way around the world, and could chew his own tail.

Fenric too was growing bigger, and more menacing,

with each passing day. And in the end – after much squealing from Sif and bellowing from Thor – even Odin found himself facing facts: Fenric would *not* make a good pet. Fenric would, in fact, do exactly what he was destined to do: end the cosmos.

'Okay, so *now* can I smash the hulking brute's head in?' Thor drawled hopefully, when Odin finally told his fellow gods of this verdict.

'Bloodshed is never a remedy,' said Odin, pretending not to see Thor boggling at him. 'We've just got to bind him to a rock or something so he can't do any harm. That'll gain us a few hundred years before he breaks free and starts Ragnarok.'

So the gods created a powerful chain of steel and said, 'Hey, Wolfy Wolfy! Does Wolfikins want to see if he can break this!'

Fenric snorted with scorn and agreed to be bound with the chain. Which he then snapped with one tug.

'Oops… er, I mean, great work, Fenric!' clapped

the gods, before dashing off to create a brand new chain ten times as thick. 'Come on Big Fella, you can do it!' they cheered as they bound him to the rock again.

'Sure I can,' yawned Fenric, swiping at the chain with a lazy paw, and shattering it into fragments.

The rather pale-looking gods clapped weakly and rushed off to discuss what to do about this repellent monster.

'The dwarfs!' shouted Saga, after weeks of conduct unbecoming to gods – bickering, blame-spreading, and back-stabbing. 'They're pretty good at making stuff, I mean, just look at Freya's lovely necklace –'

There was an awkward silence as everyone carefully did not look at Freya turning very, very red. No one was quite sure how she'd got the dwarfs to part with such a prize, but Loki had spread some rather bawdy gossip.

* * * * *

The chain which the dwarfs sent as a response to the gods' grovelling pleas looked like… a long stringy ribbon.

'That's… IT?' bawled Sif. 'We are SO doomed!'

'It's an *enchanted* chain,' soothed Thor, reading the dwarfs' letter. 'Woven from six things that don't exist: a woman's beard, the roots of a rock, a bear's sinews, a fish's breath, the spit of a bird, and the sound of a cat's paws.'

So off all the gods trooped to tell Fenric it was time for another thrilling round of the 'bind him to a rock' game. Fenric wasn't the smartest of fellows, but he was beginning to get the fuzzy idea that his hosts didn't like him very much. He sniffed at the chain and agreed to try it… if, and only if, one of the gods put his hand inside Fenric's jaw.

There was a very long silence. Then Tir, God of Law, strode – well, tottered – bravely forward and stuck his hand into the Wolf's jaw. Then the other gods chained Fenric to the rock – and try as he may, there was no breaking free.

'So!' growled the Wolf. 'You found a chain stronger than me – at long last! Well done! You can let me go now!'

'Er...' said Odin. 'Perhaps you may like to, um, *rest* there, for... well... *ever*...?'

There was a nasty crunching sound as Tir the Law-Giver became Tir of the One Hand.

STORY 9

Medea

'Medea' based on the Greek myth of the Golden Fleece.

Introducing:

Grapheme 'le', sound /ul/ (*capable, battle, hurtle...*)

Medea

Hi! I'm Medea.

Yeah, it's NOT a common name, is it? Used to be when I was a little girl, but for some reason it's just not that popular these days...

Oh. That was your way of asking if I'm THE Medea?

Yeah, I'm THE Medea, okay? Medea the Witch, Medea the Queen, Medea the Murderess, Medea of the good ship *Argo*, Medea of a thousand tales...

What do you MEAN, did I really chop my little brother into a hundred bits and chuck him into the sea? How DARE you. I SO did not!

It was SIX bits! Maximum!

* * * * *

It all starts when Jason turns up at Daddy's court
(Daddy being the King of Colchis), looking for
some silly Golden Fleece thingy. He's every inch the
Noble Hero: tall, dark, square-jawed and just a bit
dim-looking. Naturally, I fall head-over-heels for
the loser. (I'm *sixteen*, for heaven's sake.)

The Golden Fleece is stuck on a tree at World's
End, watched over by a dragon. (Yeah, some
enchanted yellow sheep flew my granddad to
safety... and then he went and SKINNED it!)
Daddy does NOT want to hand over the Golden
Fleece... but it would be SUCH bad manners to
tell a Hero to scram. So Daddy says Jason can have
the oh-so-famous lump of wool... IF he can sow a
meadow with dragons' teeth... using fire-breathing
bulls!

So, with Jason looking utterly bamboozled, I hurtle
into his arms, promising to render him capable of
the task... *if* he'll marry me. My Beloved wobbles.
Double-takes. Turns purple. And... at last!...
mutters 'Yeah... okay... whatever. Er... what was

your name again?'

I bubble over with love and happiness.

Jason looks a bit sick, to be frank.

* * * * *

Anyway, I whip up a quick spell and ta-da – my Hero is fire-proof! Cattle harnessed, no problem! Meadow sown with hundreds of dragons' teeth! Oops… dragons' teeth growing into hundreds of men keen to do battle! Jason chucks a handful of pebbles into the middle of the men (no, he's not that quick-thinking – I gave him those pebbles… just in case). With screams of 'Who did that?' they start to battle each other…

Daddy shuffles and snuffles… and promises to hand over the Fleece *tomorrow*. I put an ear to his door and discover he's actually gonna kill The Love Of My Life and set fire to his ship.

So I grab Jason, hurtle towards World's End, and enchant the dragon into a mellow snooze. Then I give my Hero a leg-up to grab the sheepskin. Sadly (for him!) my kid brother spots us scrambling back to the good ship *Argo*, and races along on his chubby little legs, determined not to be left out of this Exciting Adventure.

* * * * *

Alas, Daddy is soon speeding after the *Argo* with an entire *fleet* of ships! Many lamentable wails of 'We're DOOMED! Save us, oh gods!' and suchlike from Jason's rattled crew of fellow 'champions'.

The gods do zilch so it's up to me to save us all. It suddenly strikes me that if I should happen to hack my little brother to bits and chuck said bits into the sea… Daddy will have to stop to pick 'em up! No decent burial equals no happiness in the afterlife!

So I whip out my dagger… and suddenly my kid brother is taking a swim.

Well, *bits* of him are, anyway.

* * * * *

Let's get this clear: I didn't do it for FUN. Sure, I'd spent years dreaming about doing the brat in, but I didn't *mean* it. Well… not much. Well… can you *blame* me? There I was, ten years old, smart, adorable, already a remarkable witch, and in line for the crown… and then mama goes and has this screaming brat. And just cos it's a *male* brat, it gets all the cooing and the kingdom. Sickening.

As is the effect on Jason and his merry men, who leap back like I'm a leper. I mean, these men had run amok across the world. Did they think no little kids perished when they set fire to ENTIRE TOWNS? Yet suddenly they're carrying on like they're *Mahatma Gandhi* or something.

I mean – hello! – it's ME who has just lost a brother! *And* who has bloodstains *all over* my mantle that *no amount* of scrubbing *ever* gets out!

Oh, stop looking at me like that. Like *you'd* have acted any different.

* * * * *

We sail on, Jason giving me sickly grins and backing away each time I so much as try to nuzzle him. This rankles, but doesn't deter me from saving his miserable life when the Sirens pop up to sing the ship onto the rocks... *or* when Talos the Brass Titan attempts to sink us... At last, I've saved Jason's miserable life so often that he grits his teeth and sets a wedding date...

I wear a green dress that matches my eyes... *and* Jason's skin-tone after he spends the day breaking the world mead-drinking record. But this is the Most Happy Day Of My Life and no amount of retching from my bridegroom is gonna alter that.

We go on to have a couple of kids. Twin sons. Mini-Jasons. To no one's surprise, I turn out not to be the maternal kind of woman. Waving rattles over cradles... SO not my cup of tea.

* * * * *

At long last, me and my husband (*woo hoo – husband*!) make it back to his kingdom. The one that was stolen by his Wicked Uncle. Said Wicked Uncle promised to hand back the kingdom if Jason ever got his hands on the Golden Fleece. Needless to say, he attempts to wiggle out of the deal when Jason turns up (thanks to ME!) alive and kicking and waving said Fleece around.

And Jason agrees to let his uncle remain King till he keels over!

Please don't ask which bit of 'He killed my ma, he killed my pa, he nicked my kingdom' Jason has somehow failed to grasp…

Well, being a dutiful wife, I take it upon myself to deal with this little problem. I'd learnt (the hard way!) that killing one's relatives tends to be frowned upon. So instead of exterminating the Foul Murderer myself, I trick his own girls into doing it! Yes, I tell them (and *show* them, with a sheep) that if they cut Daddy up and stick him in my enchanted pot, they'll restore his long-lost youth!

Oops! I 'forget' to use the correct spell, so the Wicked Uncle remains very, VERY dead. I expect his girls' mouths to remain firmly shut about the fact they've bumped off Daddy, but they go and wail the truth to all and sundry! And the next thing, a rabble is hammering down the palace gates, baying for MY blood! AND Jason's! We have to retreat pretty sharpish, I can tell you.

(That's the same fickle rabble who'd just been cheering us to the roof-tops, for heaven's sake.)

* * * * *

We flee to the next-door kingdom, whose King is happy to welcome us. A bit too happy, in fact. He actually has the cheek to offer Jason his girl to wed!

Well, My Darling does all the double-taking, turning-purple stuff he did on that happy day I proposed to him. I wait for him to tell the Shameless Hussy and the Shameless Hussy's kingly dad that – hello! – he *already has* an adorable wife so they can both stuff it.

Instead of which, Jason says yes.

Ever had one of those moments? When the world
keeps turning and the men keep jabbering and the
birds keep making stupid tweet-tweet sounds? As if,
between one breath and the next, your past, your
tomorrows, your heart, your *life*, haven't shattered
into a thousand fragments? Little stabbing
fragments that make it hard to take each breath?
And hard to remember *why* you're bothering to
take each breath...?

No...? Well, you've probably got all that to look
forward to, then.

* * * * *

'Medea!' exclaims The Ex-Love Of My Life,
grabbing my hands. 'I swear you will always come
first with me! This "wedding" will merely be to get
us and the lads a home! *You* are my real wife! I don't
fancy that girl *at all*!'

By now The Traitor is trembling a bit at the look
on my face. As well he may, frankly. I smile my

sweetest smile. 'Why, dearest,' I say meekly, 'whatever you think best. I'd be a poor sort of wife if I didn't obey your every whim and fancy.'

I kid you not – The Deserter actually SWALLOWS THIS! *And* starts *preening himself* as I promise to weave his new bride a lovely wedding dress with my own fair hands, to show there are no hard feelings!

Chortle chortle! You should've seen the smirk wiped off his stupid face as the Shameless Hussy puts on the dress and – *whoosh*! – goes up in flames!

* * * * *

Well, Jason never forgives me.

No, really – *he* never forgives *me*!

We both have to get the hell out of there, fast. And then The Fickle Freak makes it quite clear that never setting eyes on me again is pretty much all he asks of life now that his Poor Darling is a big pile of ashes. (Yeah, so much for 'I don't fancy that girl *at all*!', eh?)

No, I *didn't* murder my kids and fly away on a dragon! Hell's bells! You slice up one member of your family and suddenly everyone claims it's some sort of *habit*! And do I *look* as if I own any dragons…?

No, I've no idea what happened to the brats. They had Jason's piggy little eyes in insipid little faces. Let him take care of them.

* * * * *

Oh, you haven't heard what happens to Jason? It's PRICELESS! Maybe there *are* justice-loving gods in the heavens after all – cos he never has a moment's luck after he abandons me. My Ex-Hero turns into a tramp and ambles aimlessly around for years until he bumps into the good ship *Argo*. 'You're my only – *hic*! – chum!' slurs the old drunk, before lying down for a nice snooze in the shade of said chum.

Timbers from the rotting old ship fall down and kill him. Way to go, *Argo*! I giggle my HEAD off when I hear about it.

But, oh gods, how I miss him.

MRI: Mature Reading Instruction

MRI Level 1
11 stories and plays

MRI Level 2
22 stories, plays and poems

MRI Level 3
12 stories and plays

MRI Level 4A
10 stories, plays and poems

MRI Level 4B
9 stories and plays

MRI Level 5A
5 stories and plays

MRI Level 5B
12 stories, plays and poems

MRI Lesson Plans Levels 1, 2 and 3
Easy-to-use guides which include: Comprehension and Discussion Questions, Storyboarding, Oracy, Prosody, Spelling, Basic Grammar, Vocabulary and Language Development, Phoneme Breakdown, Syllable Chunking, Word Chains, Crosswords, and Recall Quizzes.

MRI Tutor Guide
Photocopiable guide including: Practical Teaching Points, Initial and Final Assessments, Background Information About the Stories, Record Keeping, Fluency Practice, Copying and Dictation Exercises, Frequently Asked Questions, and Troubleshooting.

Visit us online at www.piperbooks.co.uk

Printed in Great Britain
by Amazon

30700507R00095